Related Events to the Second Coming of the Christ

THE RESURRECTION OF HUMANS

Guaranteed Life after Life

Volume 8

Michael W. Dewar

Copyright © 2023 by Michael W. Dewar
THE RESURRECTION OF HUMANS
Guaranteed Life after Life
Series: *Related Events to the Second Coming of the Christ*

ISBN: 979-89856973-8-4

Published by Dwelling Place Cleansing
Brooklyn, New York 11236
United States of America
DPSCleansing.com

All rights reserved solely by the author. The author guarantees all contents are original and do not infringe upon the legal rights of any other person or work. No part of this book may be reproduced in any form without the permission of the author.

Unless otherwise indicated, Bible quotations are taken from The Holy Bible, New International Version(NIV). Copyright © 1973, 1978, 1984 by International Bible Society; The Holy Bible, King James Version(KJV); and The Holy Bible, New Living Translation(NLT). Copyright © 1996 by Tyndale House Publishers, Inc.

Dedication

This book is dedicated to all my nieces and nephews with the hope they will all be in the resurrection of life on that great day.

"For as in Adam all die, even so in Christ shall all be made alive" (1Cor.15:22 KJV).

CONTENTS

PREFACE vii
INTRODUCTION 9
CHAPTER 1 15
UNDERSTANDING SIN AND DEATH 15
CHAPTER 2 27
SPIRITUAL RESURRECTION 27
CHAPTER 3 35
IMMORTALITY OF THE SOUL 35
CHAPTER 4 45
RESURRECTION OF THE BODY 45
CHAPTER 5 53
BELIEVERS' RESURRECTION 53
CHAPTER 6 67
UNBELIEVERS' RESURRECTION 67
CHAPTER 7 75

ETERNAL LIFE	75
REFERRENCES	83
ABOUT THE AUTHOR	85
OTHER BOOKS BY THIS AUTHOR	87

PREFACE

Much has been said already in this series concerning the end-time resurrections of mortals, therefore, this volume is at risk for redundancy. But it is a risk I am willing to take because the volume pulls together in one place, just about everything on resurrection, making it easier to study the subject. That is the purpose for this resurrection volume.

Volume 3 (*The Great Tribulation Survival Guide...*) of the series was first written. Yes, written before the series was decided upon. For that reason, some of that material on resurrection is revisited in this volume and volume 1 as well.

The focus of this volume, as the cover indicates, is the end-time resurrection of all human beings: the righteous and unrighteous.

The resurrection of Jesus Christ guarantees the resurrection of all humans. The word of God assures us that "as in Adam all die, so in Christ shall all be made alive" (1Cor.15:22). This promise is the nexus or interconnection of the resurrection of all humans.

As surely as the rebellion of Adam brings death upon all, even so the obedience of Christ brings the promise of life upon all the sons of Adam and the daughters of Eve, whether they are believers or unbelievers. In other words, all mortals are destined to die, and all dead mortals are destined to rise and live again.

But believers and unbelievers will not be raised from the dead at the same time, and they are not appointed for the same judgment session nor destination. The righteous will be sent to a happy place. But the unrighteous will be sent to a place where there will be weeping and gnashing of teeth (Matt.8:10-12).

Each person with the breath of life has a huge stake in this matter. The stock price could not be higher, but the company has paid for our shares. All we need to do is accept the gift of God, and sign for it (John 3:16). The company is amazingly generous!

Therefore, since each of us has a vested interest as to how the shares are allocated, the more knowledge we possess about the investments made on our behalf, the better able we are to mitigate the risk and loss (John 3:14-18).

Jesus informs us that the kingdom of heaven is like a treasure hidden in a field, when a person finds it…, he sells all that he has and acquires the field. Some humans will receive and retain this treasure, while others will reject it and suffer loss. The treasure of eternal life is given to all humans, but some will reject it and suffer great loss (v.16).

These issues should make this study on human resurrection truly illuminating, edifying, and interesting. I hope you and others with use this volume and the others in the series to conduct study groups all over the world.

INTRODUCTION
The Word of Life

The Word of God, written or spoken, is life-giving. Jesus said, "...the words that I speak to you are spirit, and they are life" (John 6:63 NKJV). For this reason, Genesis, the book of beginnings, opens with God speaking things into existence, and the life-giving Spirit of God hovers the waters of creation (Gen.1:1-26). The key creative phrase in this first chapter of Genesis is, "And God said." It signals that His word is the creative life-giving agent of all things.

The Son of God whom we come to know as Jesus Christ in the New Testament (NT), was very much there in Genesis as the preincarnate Word and Agent of creation. In other words, the Son was there creating with the Father and the Holy Spirit. Creation is the work of the blessed Holy Trinity. How do we know this?

The apostle John tells us, "In the beginning was the Word, and the Word was with God, and the Word was God. He was in the beginning with God. Through him all things were made; without him nothing was made that has been made"(John 1:1-2). John goes on to say, "In him was life, and that life was the light of all mankind" (v.3). But John did not stop here, he advanced another step.

He declares, "The Word became flesh and made his dwelling among us. We have seen his glory, the glory of the one and only Son, who came from the Father, full of grace and truth" (v.14). John is saying that the preincarnate, creative Word of Genesis became incarnate in the person of Jesus Christ of Nazareth (Luke 1:26-35).

The God of creation is not only about originating life by bringing it into existence through the agency of His Word (His Son), but He gives life and eternal life to dead things and dead people.

Jesus identifies Satan, sin, and death as enemies of God and His creation. Speaking of Satan Jesus said, "The thief comes only to steal and kill and destroy…" (John 10:10a). When you compare these words with what happened to our ancestral parents with Satan in the Paradise Garden, you will see why Jesus labels Satan as a thief, a killer, and a destroyer (Gen.3:1-24).

Three Enemies

The outcome of sin, death, and Paradise loss for the human family are all traceable to Satan and his deception of the woman and the man in Eden. These three: Satan, sin, and death are enemies of God and the human family. They are a tag-team, inextricably bound together. But Christ through His death on the cross and triumphant resurrection defeated all three for the human family.

We will briefly look at these three enemies in this section. But before we do, let us go back to John 10:10 and read the second half of the verse. Jesus speaking, "[But] I have come that they may have life and have it to the full." Or, have life "more abundantly"(KJV). Abundant life, fullness of life, and eternal life are the same.

The first half of the verse reveals Satan's mission. It is to destroy the human family with sin and death and take them to hell with him. Hell is the place of eternal death or separation. The Bible also calls hell "the second death" (Rev.20:6). Those who live or die without eternal life in Christ will perish in this place (John 3:16).

Second, the mission of Jesus Christ is stated in the second half of the verse (John 10:10b). It is to give abundant life or fullness of life to the human family. That is to give eternal life through His death and resurrection to humans that they might escape the second death, the eternal place of separation (Matt.20:28; John 3:14-18). Christ's mission is accomplished in two phases.

The first phase of Christ's mission is to provide redemption for the human family by His death and resurrection. By the cross, Christ nullifies the power of sin, Satan, and death (Matt.1:21; Heb.2:9-11). These three enemies are still around, but their powers are broken. In relation to sin, the word of God declares, "sin shall not have dominion over you [the believer in Christ]" (Rom.6:14). Why?

Because sin's power has been broken, and the believer now has the indwelling Holy Spirit and the Word of God to live victoriously. Jesus under the power of the Holy Spirit and the Word faced Satan in the wilderness temptations, and told him, "It is written" three times (Matt.4:1-10).

In relation to Satan, Jesus defeated Satan at the cross; as the Seed of the Woman, Jesus crushed the serpent's head and nullifies his power (Gen.3:15; Heb.2:9-11). For this reason, the Word of God instructs believers not to run from Satan, but to stand their ground and resist the devil and the devil will flee from them (Eph.6:10-17; James 4:7; 1Peter 6 8-9). For the Holy Spirit who dwells in the believer is greater than Satan who dwells in world (1 John 4:4).

In relation to death, the third enemy, Jesus conquered death by His resurrection, so death has no more dominion over Him. The apostle Paul gives us this intelligence report: "For we know that since Christ was raised from the dead, he cannot die again; death no longer has mastery over him. The death he died, he died to sin once for all; but the life he lives, he lives to God" (Rom.6:9-10).

The critical point to remember is this: Jesus did not die for Himself, he died for us, humankind. His death was a sacrifice to God for our redemption (Isa.53:1-12; Rom.5:12-21). Sin produces death, not just spiritual and physical death but eternal death. Jesus conquered death by resurrection; that means, he conquers death and guarantees resurrection for the entire human family. For this reason, the Word of God declares, "As in Adam all die, even so in Christ shall all be made alive" (1Cor.15:22 KJV).

Note carefully what the preceding verse is saying. Because of Adam's sin and our own sins, all humans die; that is the natural outcome of sin. But note again that the verse says, "even so in Christ shall all be made alive." Jesus Christ, the sinless, righteous One secures forgiveness of sin for us and guarantees resurrection for all. But do not jump for joy yet, for there is another critical point to understand in this redemptive transaction.

The death of Christ secures *pardon for sin* for all human beings, that "whosoever believes in Him should not perish but have eternal life" (John3:16). Within this promised gift of everlasting or eternal life is our coming back from death. I stated earlier that the sacrifice of Christ secures forgiveness or pardon from sin. But a pardon is not effective until it is accepted. So, only those people who accepts God's gift of salvation receives forgiveness of sin.

For example, the governor of a State or the President of the United States can pardon anyone, even someone sentenced to death. But that pardon is useless if the person it is offered to refuses it. The person on death row remains under condemnation if he refuses the pardon offered to him.

In like manner, Jesus died to pardon every human being but only the whosoever believes in Him will not perish benefit, because they are the ones that accept the pardon God offers (John 3:16; Rom.6:23). To believe is to accept pardon and receive eternal life. There is one more critical point to understand.

Remember the First Corinthian passage quoted earlier? It also says, "so in Christ shall all be made alive" (15:22). Whether a person receives Christ's pardon or not, all human beings will die because of sin and all human beings will rise again from the dead because of Christ's death and resurrection.

But all humans will not rise from the dead at the same time because there is a resurrection order (vv.20-23). Furthermore, all resurrected humans do not go to the same destination; believers go to heaven where they are judged and rewarded for their works (1 Thess.4:13-18; 2Cor.5:10). But unbelievers are judged for their sins and sent to hell, the destination they chose (Rev.20:11-15).

Individuals who accept Christ pardon before they die physically, will rise to eternal life (destination heaven). But those that reject the pardon offered to them will die as unbelievers and rise again to eternal death (destination hell). The connection between sin and all three levels of death is clear in scripture for the unbeliever.

But now we are faced with a new question on death as it relates to the believer: why are believers' death necessary? We come into this world under the sentence of death, and by accepting Christ sacrifice, pardon, and forgiveness, we crossover from death to life. Since Christ paid the penalty of sin and death for us, why is it necessary for believers to go through the harrowing experience of death and bereavement all over again that Christ has suffered it on our behalf? The Bible does not speak of the believers' death in harrowing terms. We will return to this question later.

Summary

This is the sum of the matter. By reason of the death and resurrection of Christ, all humans, good and bad will rise again from the dead. But they will not all be rising at the same time or be going to the same place. Some will rise to the resurrection of life, while others rise to be condemned (John 5:28). That is what the Bible means when it says, "The wages of sin is death, but the gift of God is eternal life through Jesus Christ our Lord" (Rom.6:23).

The eternal destination of the resurrected is determined by the individual's relationship with Jesus Christ while he or she was alive in the physical body. If the person lived selfishly, serving sin and Satan, his or her wages is death as reflected in the preceding quote. All these themes are discussed with detail in this book.

Again, this introduction has touched on several themes relating to sin and death, believers and unbelievers, resurrection, and eternal destination. These themes will be discussed in more detail through this book. The reader is also referred to Volume 1 and 9 in this series for added insights.

CHAPTER 1

UNDERSTANDING SIN AND DEATH

To understand Christian thought on human resurrection, you must first come to understand the biblical concept of sin and death. The introduction has already given the fundamentals on these mysterious entities. All that is said throughout the rest of this book depends on what is said in the introduction. In this chapter we discussed sin, and three types of death. We also looked at the death and resurrection of Jesus Christ and their immeasurable impact upon human life, death, and resurrection. We begin with a discussion on sin because it is the root cause of death.

What Is Sin?

The Word of God is the final authority on sin, not popes, bishops, priests, pastors, or anyone else. The Word defines sin, tells us why it is offensive to God, dangerous to humans, its penalty, and its remedy. Sin is a mysterious entity, a communicable, viral disease of the soul. Sin is a spiritual disease; it is to the soul, body, and mind what a deadly virus, like Ebola, COVID-19 or cancer is to the human body. Sin has one hundred percent fatality; all humans have acquired it and all humans will die because of it (Rom.5:12).

Like a cancer that metastases to destroy the host--sin destroys the whole person, body, and soul in hell. Hell is the place of death, eternal death, or separation from God. The word of God informs us that the "wages of sin is death" (Rom.6:23).

But what has been said thus far describes what sin does; it does not define it. So, let us give it a biblical definition. "Sin is the transgression of the law," God's law (1John 3:4-6). This definition of sin is short, but certainly not simple. The word "transgression" is more than a light infraction; it is rebellion against God. "Sin is lawlessness," a person putting his will and desires above the will of God (1 Thess.2:7-12). All humans have this inclination or struggle.

In Gethsemane, Jesus was moved to put His human will above the will of His Father. Plainly, the devil tried to get Him to sin (Matt.26:36-42). This is Satan's *modus aperandi*, his native way of doing things, whether he is tempting Adam and Eve or Jesus. This is the same approach believers face when tempted, a struggle between our will versus the will of God. The will of God is expressed in His Word. His Words are executive orders, laws to be obeyed, not suggestions to be ignored.

Every kingdom or nation operates by law. Law is supposed to bring harmony, justice, and peace to a society; thus, the saying, no justice, no peace! Justice and peace are inextricably bound together. God is the supreme lawgiver, and His principles of divine law were operable among humans from creation. But were not placed in writing until the time of Moses.

The written text of God's law was handed down on Mount Sinai to humans by Moses (Exod.19-20). These laws, though given to the Israelites, were intended as the rules for living for all peoples and nations on the earth (Gen.12:1-3).

The societies that live by the Law of God will have harmony, justice restrained by mercy, and human flourishing. But societies or nations that discard God's Law will not do well. To some measure, they will enjoy the blessings of God's *common grace*. But persistent rebellion against God leads to destruction. "Righteous exalts a nation, but sin is a reproach to any people" (Prov.14: 34).

Again, the Law was given to Israel not just for Israel's sake but as a vehicle of blessing to all nations upon the earth. Israel was chosen as the conduit, covenant nation, the model nation for the rest of the world. Through Israel the Messiah would come as the full revelation of God to all humankind. Israel waited with great expectation for the arrival of this promised leader.

An old man named Simeon testified that God promised that he would not die until he sees the Christ child, the Messiah. Simeon holding the child Jesus uttered this blessing, "Sovereign Lord as you have promised, you may now dismiss your servant in peace. For my eyes have seen your salvation, which you have prepared in the sight of all nations; a light for revelation to the Gentiles, and the glory of thy people Israel" (Luke 2:28-32). Note that the coming of the Christ child through Israel would be a blessing to all nations on the earth.

But Israel reneged on their covenant responsibility by not keeping the terms of the covenant which are clearly laid out in the Torah and summarized in Deuteronomy 28 under the blessings of obedience and the curse of disobedience. From Judges to Malachi, Israel's history is one of going counter to the covenant they agreed to—they reneged and inherited the curse.

But to add insult to injury, Israel rejected the Messiah when He arrived among them; they had him executed by crucifixion as a common criminal (John 1:12, 18:1-40, 19:1-42). For these reasons among others, God raised up the Church to bring the revelation of His Word and salvation to the entire world (Matt.28:19-20).

You will observe that the Nations of the world that embrace the Christian message, the revelation of God, are the nations that thrive and flourish and are among leading world powers. Where the Word of God has taken root, people tend thrive and flourish above those where it is rejected or suppressed. Bradley G. Green observes that wherever the gospel has taken roots, the academy follows.[1] Jesus invites His followers to come and learn from Him (Matt.11:28-29).

The Gospel, the light of God, the revelation of God, dispels the darkness of ignorance, superstition, and backwardness wherever it is allowed to shine. Schools like Harvard, Yale, and Princeton were founded to train ministers for the Church, the liberal arts followed.

Sin is lawlessness, rebellion against God. It is pernicious, and God will judge all persons that transgress His law and sentence them to a just punishment. Since all humans are sinners and stand guilty before God under the sentence of death, unless someone serves our sentence, we must (Rom.2:9-13).

God provides someone to take the sentence of death for the human family and thereby pardons everyone. That is what Jesus did on the cross, by His death and resurrection. God issued a pardon for everyone (John 3:16). But remember, a pardon is not effective until it is accepted. When a person rejects Jesus Christ, he or she rejects the only pardon for sin God offers through His Son (Matt.1:21; John 3:16-18). Salvation from sin is offered nowhere else (Acts 4:12). God has one salvation plan for all people.

If a person rejects pardon until physical death comes to him or her, that person is eternally lost. Isaiah admonished the people of Israel, "Seek the Lord while he may be found; call upon him while he is near. Let the wicked forsake their ways and the unrighteous their thoughts. Let them turn to the Lord, and he will have mercy on them...for he will freely pardon" (Isa.55:6-7).

Whether a person lived in the Old Testament (OT) era or is currently living in the New Testament (NT) period, to reject God's offer of pardon is to perish (John 3:16). Perish here refers to eternal separation from God.

Arrogant people always want to redeem themselves, but we have nothing to offer God for our redemption, so God chose to pay the high cost for us. But if we reject God's offer, that leaves one alternative, we pay the price for our sin. The price is death, physical death, and eternal death in hell (John 3:16; Rom.6:23).

But before the rejector of salvation goes to hell, God will have him or her resurrected from physical death to stand trial, then sent off to serve the sentence given. That sentence is eternal death. The Bible has made it clear repeatedly that the sentence will be eternal for those who reject pardon, and the blessing will be eternal life for those who accept God's pardon and gift of salvation. Again, take note, eternal death, and eternal life.

Understanding Death

The Bible speaks of three types of deaths: spiritual death, physical death, and eternal death. Death can also be spoken of as one entity with three stages because one must end before the other begins.

In the previous section, sin is defined as the transgression of God's law, as rebellion against God, as lawlessness. The skeleton summary of God's Law is the *Ten Commandments*; the full text of God's Law is the whole Bible, also called the Word of God. It is set forth in two covenants or Testaments, Old and New.

Some ceremonial laws of the Old Covenant are no longer applicable under the New Covenant. Other than that, "All Scripture is given by inspiration of God, and is profitable for doctrine, for reproof, for correction, for instruction in righteousness, that the man of God might be complete, thoroughly equipped for every good work" (2 Tim.3:16-17 NKJV).

In other words, the Word of God is the complete toolkit or instruction manual for the spiritual life; it is the constitution of the Kingdom of God as it relates to humankind. The Word of God is the final rule or authority for the Christian faith and practice.

No human has the authority to overrule the Word of God, whether he be bishop or pope, cardinal or priest, or deacon or pastor, not even angels have that authority (Gal.1:8-9,11-12). The Bible, the Word of God, is His standard for human life and conduct.

The Word of God occupies the place of centrality among the people of God. It defines human relationship to God, to other humans, to angels, other created beings, animals, and the creation itself. The Word of God set forth human responsibilities or duties to God and neighbor. The first four commandments summarize our duty to God and the other six our duties to neighbor (Ex.20:1-17; Deu.5:6-21). The duties were ratified, clarified, and expanded upon by Jesus Christ in the Sermon on the Mount (Matt.5-7).

Therefore, when we speak of death as it relates to humans who are the image bearer of God, we must do so in the light of the Word of God. The giver of life is the one who defines life and death.

So, what is death as it relates to humans? Death is as mysterious as life. The answer depends upon a question asked by the Psalmist, "What is man?" (Psalm 8: 1-8 KJV). The Word of God teach that Humans are both physical and spiritual beings created in God's image and likeness (Gen.1:27-28). We are created not just different but superior to the brute, beast creation.

Therefore, death is not the end of human existence, but a mere change of condition and place but conscious existence continues (Unger 1988, 379).[2] In the gospel of Luke (16:19-31), Jesus speaks of two men who knew each other in life and continued conscious existence, recognition, and communication after death. Jesus also called back his friend Lazarus to life who had been dead and buried for four days. Jesus called him by name, and he responded (John 11:38-44). The implication is that Lazarus was dead to humans, but alive somewhere and was able to respond to the command of Jesus Christ to come back, and he did come back.

Some people are quick to say, that is absurd! Yes, to some extent it is absurd. But the Almighty is not boxed in or limited by what humans consider absurd. God is free to exercise His power whenever and wherever He sees fit.

Let us zoom in more closely on the three levels of death. The Bible teaches that death in all three levels is not the cessation of conscious existence, but separation from God. We will return to this point of *conscious existence* later.

Some scripture passages speak of death as if it is a living entity. It is called, "the last enemy;" it has a "sting," and God will destroy it (1 Cor.15: 55-56). This implies ontological status, that it has being, consciousness or will. It also has a mission and that is to stay around until the last son of Adam and last daughter of Eve is put down. "For as in Adam all die…" (v. 22).

So, what is death? Simply stated, death in all three stages (spiritual, physical, and eternal) is "separation" from God. Spiritual death is separation of the human soul and spirit from God (Eph.2:1-5). The person is cut off from fellowship or spiritual life with God.

Spiritual life is like branches on a tree; branches die when detached from their life source. In like manner, the human soul or spirit is in a state of spiritual death when cut off from its life source (John 15:1-6). As a blind man is dead to seeing, and a deaf man is dead to hearing, so is the one who is spiritually dead. He is physically alive, but the soul/spirit is cut-off from God.

You may further note that our ancestral parents in the Paradise Garden suffered spiritual death before physical death took them away. The command given to the man and his wife was not to eat of a particular tree for if eaten they would surely die (Gen.2:16-17). The moment they engaged in that act of sin, rebellion, lawlessness and ate, they were cut off from fellowship with God.

The glory of God that covered them departed; they observed that they were naked and were ashamed and hid themselves. That is spiritual death, separation from God (Gen.3:1-13). But physical death did not come to the man and his wife until a few hundred years later. In fact, Adam lived a total of 930 years, then he died physically (Gen.5:1-5).

Like Adam, spiritual death comes to all humans first, because we were born in sin, soul and spirit separated from God. That is why we need to be born again (John 3:1-8). Jesus is the only human that had no sin; He had no earthly father that connects Him to Adam. Jesus is the only human who is the seed of the woman (Gen.3:15). His mother was still a Virgin when Jesus was born (Luke 1:26-38). We are all the seed of the man; we carry the poison of death in us.

Physical death is the separation of the soul/spirit from the body after all functions ceased: heart stops, breathing is terminated, and brain activity is no more. The soul/spirit has exited the body; it is absent from the body. That is physical death; it is to be permanently absent from the body, yet consciously present somewhere else. Is that possible? The word of God answers.

Let me emphasize, in physical death, the soul/spirit is gone from the body but is conscious and alive with God. The body is dead and subject to decay. The soul/spirit is with God but that does not necessarily mean in a happy place. Spiritual death is to God what a physically dead person is to us. The former is cutoff from God, yet alive to us, whereas the latter is cutoff from us but alive to God. In physical death the person has put off his earth suit, he is "absent from the body" but present with the Lord (2 Cor.5:1-6). The soul can be with God, yet not in a happy place. We will revisit this point.

Eternal death is permanent separation of the whole person, body, and soul/spirit from God in hell (Matt.10:28; Rev.20:11-15).

Conquering Death to Live Eternally

"The wages of sin is death but the gift of God is eternal life through Jesus Christ our Lord" (Rom.6:23). Eternal life is not a gift you receive after you are dead; it is a gift to be received through knowing Jesus while you are alive in the physical body (John 3:16).

If you wait until you die physically to receive the gift of eternal life, you miss it completely, and you are eternally lost (John 3:16-18). We are born into this world already lost. The Bible teaches that "the Son of Man came to seek and to save that which was lost (Matt.18:11 KJV). Jesus' mission is to give eternal life (John 10:10b).

To possess eternal life with God, a person must conquer all three stages of death, and it must be done in this life before physical death occurs. All humans have an appointment with death (Heb.9:27 KJV). The Bible tells us that death is pronounced on all Adam's children (Rom.5:12; 1Cor.15:22a). But no human can conquer death at any stage on his own; a dead man cannot help himself. Even believers in Christ were all dead in sin, separated from God (Eph.2:1-6). We needed a champion who could conquer death for us. This is where Jesus Christ comes in as our substitute to do the heavy lifting for us (Isa.53: 4-12; Matt.1:21; John 3:16).

Jesus died for our redemption on the cross, and He rose from the dead for our justification (Rom.5:1-5; Eph.1:7; Col.1:13-14). No other human being before Him had ever done that or has done it since. By His resurrection, Jesus guarantees resurrection for all humankind. "For as in Adam all die, even so in Christ shall all be made alive" (1Cor.15:22 KJV).

The good news is this—we only need to conquer spiritual death. Because by conquering spiritual death, we conquer death in all three phases. But we must do it during our earthly life before we die physically. Why is that so important? There is no repentance in the grave. The Bible teaches no intermediate place called, Purgatory, where humans can make things right to get into heaven. Purgatory is a fictitious place invented by the Roman Catholic church; it does not exist! If you die physically without a born-again experience of God's redeeming grace, you are permanently lost.

Again, if we die physically while in a state of spiritual death, we automatically inherit eternal death in hell. Without Jesus, we perish (John 3:16). It is not the fires of hell that make things horrible, it is the separation from God. He is the source of all life, the only hope for redemption. The Word of God is clear on the matter—no one can change his lost status after physical death has occurred.

Eternal life with God is offered to us while we are alive in the body. If we die without receiving this gift of God through Christ, we are forever lost (John 3:16-18). "For the wages of sin is death but the gift of God is eternal life through Jesus Christ our Lord" (Rom.6:23). Eternal life is a gift to be received before we exit the body. That gift is Jesus Christ; a gift is intended to be received. Eternal life is resident in the person of Jesus Christ only (John 3:14-18). Salvation from sin can be found in none other (Acts 4:12).

You cannot bypass Jesus and receive eternal life or go to heaven. You cannot get out of spiritual death without being joined to Jesus Christ. This process is called by different names: being born again, saved, converted, regenerated, or spiritually resurrected. The Holy Spirit works with the repentant person to bring this change about. We will discuss resurrection in the next chapter. Let us summarize what we have discussed in this chapter.

Summary

We have discussed two interrelated enemies of every human being: sin, and death. We are all sinners, and we are all under the sentence of death until we come to salvation in Christ (John 3:16-18).

The sentence of sin and death is eternal separation from God in hell (John 3:16). One word defines death, and it is separation; that is separation from God. Death has three stages of separation: spiritual, physical, and eternal.

Once we join ourselves to Jesus Christ we are lifted out of spiritual death, and we conquer the other two stages because Jesus by His cross and resurrection conquered them all for us.

Christ conquering death for believers does not mean believers will not face physical death; it means, physical death cannot permanently hold on to them. It was unable to hold on to Jesus because He proved to be more powerful than death.

Jesus is God's gift of salvation from sin, death, and hell (John 3:14-18; Rom.6:23; Eph.2:8). To reject Jesus is to reject salvation, refuse pardon for sin, and abide in the state spiritual death.

Spiritual death terminates in physical death, and physical death terminates in eternal death. It is like the stream ends in the river, and the river ends in the sea or ocean. To avoid eternal death, a person must repent and come to Christ before physical death comes to him or her. There is no repenting after physical death.

The only escape route from death is through Jesus Christ who said, "I am the way the truth and the life..." (John 14:6). Salvation through Jesus Christ is the gift of God, available only through Jesus Christ our Lord (John 3:16; Acts 4:12; Rom.6:23).

CHAPTER 2

SPIRITUAL RESURRECTION

There is only one way to conquer death and that is by resurrection. But no dead person can resurrect himself. Only Jesus has such ability because He is the God-Man. That means He is truly God and truly man at the same time. As Man He died but as God He lives and was able to raise Himself from the dead. Of course, the Father and the Holy Spirit also participated in His resurrection.

Jesus once said to His enemies, "Destroy this temple and I will raise it up in three days" (John2:18-22). In other words, you kill me, and I will raise myself from the dead in three days. They did kill Him on Good Friday but on Easter Sunday He was raised from the dead

(John 19 38-42, 20: 1-29). He demonstrated His capability of raising Himself from the dead.

In all of history, no other person has ever been raised from dead in the manner of Christ's resurrection. Jesus did something that no one has duplicated, and by it he guarantees resurrection for the entire human family. All humans are under the sentence of death. "For as in Adam all die, even so in Christ shall all be made alive" (Rom.5:12; 1Cor.15:22). Note the key word, all. This tells us that death is universal, and resurrection is universal.

The critical thing to know is this—all humans will not be resurrected at the same time, and all humans will not be going to the same place after resurrection. We will return to this later.

In chapter1, we discussed three types or stages of death: spiritual death, physical death, and eternal death. It follows that resurrection must also deal with all three phases of death. So, is there a spiritual resurrection, a physical resurrection, and an eternal resurrection? The short answer is yes. This chapter answers the spiritual resurrection question. Chapter 3 addresses the physical resurrection issue, and Chapter 4, the eternal resurrection.

Spiritual Resurrection

Frankly, we have already answered the question of spiritual resurrection in Chapter 1, but at the risk of being redundant we must revisit the subject from a slightly different angle.

Spiritual resurrection takes place when we repent of our sins, receive God's forgiveness, and are joined to Jesus Christ, the source of all spiritual life (John 3:1-18). The Bible uses different words to describe this resurrection status: being saved, being born-again, converted, regenerated, and so on. The apostle Paul gives us the following intelligence report on spiritual resurrection:

> And you He made alive, who were dead in trespasses and sins, in which you once walked according to the course of this world, according to the prince of the power of the air, the spirit who now works in the sons of disobedience, among whom also we all once conducted ourselves in the lust of our flesh, fulfilling the desires of the flesh and of the mind, and were by nature children of wrath, just like the others.
> But God, who is rich in mercy, because of His great love with which he loved us, even when we were dead in in trespasses, made us alive together with Christ (by grace you have been saved), and raised us up together, and made us sit together in the heavenly places in Christ Jesus, that in the ages to come He might show the exceeding riches of His grace in His kindness toward us in Christ Jesus.
> For by grace you have been saved through faith, and that not of ourselves; it is the gift of God…. (Ephesian 2:1-9 NKJV)

The preceding quote is loaded with valuable information on the spiritual life, but we do not have the space in this small book to unpack it all but note the three things that follow.

(1) The apostle is peaking to believers who were once in the state of spiritual death and are now alive from that state of death.

(2) During their former state of death, they were controlled by Satan and could not help themselves. It is God who is riche in mercy, love, grace, and kindness that got them out of that dead situation.

(3) Now they are not only raised from the dead, but they are also seated with Christ who rescued them from death in heavenly places. But how did this all happen?

The Process of Spiritual Resurrection

When the gospel message is presented to a person, the Holy Spirit convicts that person of his or her sins, the person repents, and asks Jesus for forgiveness. By doing that, pardon is issued and accepted (John 3:16). If the person is sincere, a miraculous transformation takes place in his or her life. From here onward the person belongs to God. We commonly say, you are born again, you are a believer, you have cross over from death to life (John 3:1-18).

But being born again is not as simple as it appears. Behind the scenes, God through Christ is doing most of the heavy lifting for us. This volume is too small to explain it all. I will briefly touch on three important things: sanctification, justification, and eternal life.

Sanctification. This is a noun; the verb is sanctified, and it means to make clean or holy. The moment you repent of your sins and receive Jesus as your Savior and Lord, you are forgiven and sanctified. By itself, sanctification is a huge subject. Again, it simply means, you are made holy or clean, set apart for God's purpose.

Being sanctified is not a one-time event; it is an event with process. It is like the first time you washed your dirty hands; that was an event. But since that you keep washing your hands every time it gets dirty; that is a process. Christians do get dirty repeatedly, so we get clean again and again.

Another way to explain it is to say we grow up in our sanctification. When we are first saved, we say we are born again into the kingdom of God (John 3:1-5). All newborns get dirty easily, we even defecate on ourselves, but we grow up from infancy to adult maturity and no longer get dirty so easily. And if we get dirty, we know what to do to clean up or sanctify ourselves. The same thing is true in a spiritual sense.

Note something else, a normally born child has all the parts of an adult: one head, two eyes, two ears, two hands, two feet, and the like. But the child must learn to use them over time. To God, a born-again person is perfect but from a human perspective that child needs to grow to spiritual maturity in Christ (2 Peter 3:18).

Justification. This is a noun; the verb is justified. Justification is another huge subject. It means, God has declared you righteous based on what Jesus Christ did for you on the cross (Rom.5:1-5). God the judge has acquitted you of all charges. Justification is what God does for us; it is God that justifies (Rom.8:33).

When a person receives Jesus Christ as his or her savior and Lord, God the Father acting as judge, pounds the gavel in the court of heaven acquitting the repentant sinner based on the sacrifice of Jesus, the Son of God.

Eternal Life. This is hard to grasp because it is almost too good to be true. But it is true! When the Bible says, God loves us, it is no joke, He really does. The moment we truly repent and accept Jesus Christ, we are given eternal life right here, right now (John 3:16). This gift of eternal life must be received while we are alive in the physical body. If you wait until you die, you lose your chance to receive this gift, and you will perish (John3:16).

You cannot have eternal life if you wait until you die. The Roman Catholics have it wrong! There is no purgatory, no intermediate place to make it right after you die. Jesus said to the thief on the cross who turned to Him for help, "...today you will be with me in paradise" (Luk3 23:43). What happened to the other thief; he is forever lost. Dying without knowing Jesus Christ as Savior is a serious matter. It is an issue to settle early in life (Ecc.12:1-7).

Spiritual resurrection is God's response to spiritual death. All human beings are born into this world spiritually dead because of sin. The human soul or spirit is cut-off from God. It is like there is a firewall between the Divine Spirit (God) and the human spirit preventing communication and fellowship. The Bible calls this state of being or separation, death. It also refers to the person in this state as "the natural man." He cannot understand the things of God for they are spiritually discerned; he is blinded by Satan, the god of this world (2 Cor.4:3-4).

The Word of God confirms that we were all born in sin and sharpen in iniquity, that there is none righteous, not one, we have all sinned and come short of the glory of God (Rom.2:10-18). We all remain in this state of spiritual death, waiting to be spiritually resurrected. We are resurrected to life when we respond to the gospel message and with the aid of the blessed Holy Spirit accept Jesus as our Savior and Lord.

The Saving Process

Here is the process of spiritual resurrection. Upon hearing the message of the gospel, the Holy Spirit begins to convict the person of his or her lost condition and creates saving faith in the person's heart. The person begins to see the need for change; this is call, repentance. Sometimes the change is dramatic like that of the dying thief of the cross, or that of the Ethiopian Eunuch, or that of Saul on the Damascus Road (Luke 23:32,39-43; Acts 8:26-39, 9:1-22). Other times, the change process is longer, and less dramatic.

When the repentant person submits to the Holy Spirit's prodding, and receives God's forgiveness, we say, the person is born again into the kingdom of God (John 3:1-6).

This born-again experience always results in the person embracing Jesus Christ as his or her Savior and Lord (vv.16-18). There are cases that the person resist the Holy Spirit and does not embrace Jesus as Savior and Lord (Acts 24:22-25). In this case the person abides in spiritual death until another chance comes his way. If another chance does not come his way and he dies physically in that condition, he is forever lost.

What happens when a person is under conviction? It is the Holy Spirit helping him to come to a decision about Jesus Christ. If the person cries out to God for mercy and forgiveness, the gift of salvation is given (John 3:16). It is at this point that the person's soul and spirit are quickened and infused with the life of God.

It is this coming alive of the soul that is referred to as spiritual resurrection. The Word of God speaks of it this way: "And you has He made alive who were dead in trespasses and sins (Eph.2:1).

Summary

In this chapter we defined sin as the transgression of God's law, as rebellion against God, and as lawlessness. We defined death as separation from *God*. And that death comes in three stages: spiritual, physical, and eternal.

In spiritual death, the person is physically alive, but the soul or spirit is cut-off or separated from God. God is the life source for all forms of life: for spiritual life, natural life, and eternal life.

Physical death is the separation of the soul or spirit from the body. This form of death we are more familiar with because we see and experience it in society frequently. At physical death, the body knows nothing, but the soul is in a state of conscious existence outside of the body under the control of God.

Eternal death is the permanent separation of the whole person from God in a place of torment after that person is judged and sentenced. Now that you have a basic understanding of death, we will briefly turn our attention to the immortality of the soul, then to the discussion of resurrection.

CHAPTER 3

IMMORTALITY OF THE SOUL

The immortality of the soul addresses two fundamental questions: does the soul or spirit of the human being exist in a conscious state after it separates from the body at death? and can the soul die or perish as the body perishes? Among other things, this chapter seeks to answer these two questions from scripture.

For resurrection to be valid, death must precede it. If physical death of human beings is permanent, resurrection is questionable, if not impossible. The word soul is used interchangeably in this chapter with the word spirit.

The Bible teaches that the soul or spirit survives the physical body; it does not cease to exist. Resurrection is a supernatural act of God reuniting the soul with the body.

Decomposition of the Body

The human body is engineered out of perishable material. When Adam and his wife through sin contracted the spiritual disease that leads to physical death, God said to the man, "dust you are and unto the dust you will return"(Gen.3:19). We know from observation that the body is decomposable and physical death begins the process until the body returns to the earth and is fully made one again with the soil from which it was taken. We also know from scientific testing and observation that a dead body knows nothing.

But by creation, humans are not singularly made of dust; the breath or spirit of the Almighty completes their creation (Gen.2:7). Elihu made this notable statement to Job, "The Spirit of God made me, and the breath of the Almighty gives me life" (Job 33:4). The breath or spirit is the immaterial part of human beings and that does not die; it survives the body.

Physical death ends our natural existence upon the earth, but surely, it does not the end the soul, according to Christian teachings based upon the scriptures. So where is the soul, is it conscious, does it carry the personality traits exhibited when the body was alive?

The Meaning of Immortality

The word immortal has a primary and a secondary meaning. In its primary sense, it applies only to God as the absolute, self-existent Being, incorporeal, uncreated, and eternal. He does not owe His existence to anyone or anything outside of Himself. He alone is immortal in the primary and absolute sense of the word.[1]

The apostle Paul speaks to this absolute God quality when he says, "God, the blessed and only Ruler, the King, and Lord of lords, who alone is immortal and who lives in unapproachable light, whom no one has seen or can see. To him be honor and might forever. Amen" (1Tim.6:15-15). The apostle is not saying, no other being shares immortality, but only God possesses immortality in the primary sense of the word. God here includes the Holy Trinity.

Other than God, all beings are created, and they owe their existence to God in every sense of the word. God has endowed some or all His creatures from humankind upward with continuous and endless existence or immortality. This includes all spirit beings: angels of every rank, and the souls of humans. Immortality in this secondary sense means that certain creatures have a beginning but no end. Two other questions beckon to us: 1) was human immortal before the fall, 2) and if yes, how does he regain it?

The Question of Immortality

The question of immortality is as old as humanity itself. Anywhere the question of death is introduced, the issue of immortality is at least implied. By divine revelation, Moses in the first book of the Torah writes about the creation of humans. In the same context, the possibility of human death and immortality are introduced.

The Creator gave humans tremendous liberty but restricted that liberty with one command for his safety. God commanded the man not to eat fruits from the tree of death because it would bring about his death (Gen.2:8-9, 5-17). From this it is fair to say, humans were not created with the seed of death. Death was afterwards acquired upon knowingly defying the Divine command not to eat the forbidden fruit.

The same narrative also demonstrates that death did not mean cessation of being but the separation of life from its primary life source which is God himself. The context further reveals that God would have confirmed humans in a state of immortality had he not fallen from the state he was created. How do we know this?

It is clearly implied in the words accompanying the banishment of humans from the paradise garden. Here is the conversation in the Godhead: "The man has now become like one of us, knowing good and evil. He must not be allowed to reach out his hand and take also from the tree of life and eat, and live forever" (Gen.3:22). With this decision Adam and his wife were driven from the paradise garden and the tree of life safeguarded (vv.23-24).

There is a second implication in the narrative of the fall—eating the forbidden fruit altered human genetic makeup, making them creatures of death, and dying. The conclusion can be drawn, therefore, that God did not want humans to live forever in his fallen, sinful state, permanently separated from his primary life source with all the hardships that accompany the fall (toiling, pain, disease, and suffering). Banishment, therefore, was an act of mercy.

Furthermore, since God has a backup plan of redemption in place from eternity, humans' separation from the primary life source would not be permanent. That means spiritual death and physical death would be temporary phenomenon. But only for persons who respond to redemption's invitation to live (Isa.55:1-7; John 3:16-18). Those refusing redemption would abide in death, thus eternal death. This is the Christian message (John 3:16).

The patriarch Job is the oldest or one of the oldest fathers of biblical antiquity; he asked the question, "If a man die, shall he live again?"(Job14:14). Although Job's position on the question appears to have evolved like many others, his final answer to the question is in the affirmative. How do we know that? Job left us this testimony, "For I know that my Redeemer lives, And He shall stand at last upon the earth; And after my skin is destroyed, this I know, That in my flesh I shall see God, Whom I shall see for myself, And my eyes shall behold, and not another" (Job 19:25-27 NKJV).

In these words of hope, Job looked away from his present suffering, even death itself to a brighter tomorrow, when his redeemer will stand upon the earth, and Job will be present to behold the Redeemer for himself. Job speaks confidently here, and affirmatively of the future resurrection when he will rise from the dead to participate. The Christian era teaches this very thing.

Other patriarchs and righteous servants of God, like Job, served God faithfully and died in hope to rise again to receive their inheritance. The implication is that the body is asleep, but the soul is alive and conscious, awaiting the resurrection of the righteous. But some patriarchs vacillate on the subject, even Job who answers the question of the afterlife in the affirmative, appears to evolve to that point of certainty. Perhaps, it is for this reason the Pharisees come to believe in the resurrection of the dead, while the Sadducees took the opposite view; yet both were of Judaism.

It is said that Abel offered to God a more excellent sacrifice than his brother Cain. God spoke well of him and even though he is dead he is still speaking (Heb.11:4). Enoch was taken away alive, not experiencing physical death the usual way as other men (v.5).

In faith, Abraham journeyed in the land of promise, but in reality, he was "looking forward to a city with foundation, whose architect and builder is God" (v.10). Jesus spoke of that city that he is preparing for the righteous of all ages (John 14:1-4). That city comes into manifestation at the close of the Bible for both the resurrected ones as well as the transformed ones (Rev. 21:1-27).

The implication is that these righteous ones are still waiting for God to make good on His promise. And He will, for God is faithful.

The writer of Hebrews gives the names of some who died in faith with the assurance that they will rise again to receive their inheritance promised by God (Heb.11:32-40).

Daniel, who faithfully served about four administrations in Babylon—concerned about his heavenly inheritance, innocently pressured a high-ranking angel to disclose more about the future than the angel had authority to reveal—in a mild rebuke the angel said to him, "As for you go your way till the end. You will rest, and then at the end of days you will rise to receive your allotted inheritance"(Dan.12:13). Physical death and resurrection are strongly implied in the angel's statement.

Insights from the New Testament

The New Testament (NT) speaks more clearly on the immortality of the soul; until now most of our references on the matter are drawn from the Old Testament (OT). If the soul survives the body that is convincing evidence of immortality in the secondary sense.

But even though the OT evidence is on the affirmative, it is not a strong as theological dogma; the NT evidence will be clearer and more compelling.

Like the OT, the NT does not explicitly state that the soul is immortal, nor does it formally set out to prove or argue the question. But in like manner, these two Testaments do not formally prove or argue for the existence of God, yet they contain overwhelming evidence of His existence. The same can be said for the immortality of the soul, especially in the second testament.

Furthermore, the NT explicitly states that Christ has brought life and immortality to light; this suggest a higher level of clarity on the matter. How has Christ brought life and immortality to light?

First, He unveils the spiritual fact of a born-again experience, a new birth which is a spiritual birth beyond the natural. It is a birth from above that qualifies humans to enter the kingdom of God (John 3:1-8). This was new light to Nicodemus, a teacher of Israel, a member of the Sanhedrin. Spiritual birth is necessary because apart from Christ, the soul is in a state spiritual death (Eph.2:1).

Second, Jesus offers eternal life to those who believe in Him (vv.14-18, 4:10-14). Jesus brought great clarity to this teaching; frankly, it is a new teaching. Eternal life is a present reality to be received before physical death comes to a person. The implication is this: a person with eternal life has not truly died, even though the soul separates from the body, and the body decays. This is the reality Jesus was trying to communicate to Martha when He said to her: "I am the resurrection and the life. The ones who believe in me will live, even though they die, and whoever lives by believing in me will never die..." (John 11:25-26).

Third, Jesus in His ministry called back people from the dead to life again in the body as He did with His friend Lazarus. Jesus said in a loud voice to Lazarus who was dead and buried for four days, "Lazarus, come out!" (John 11:43-44). Surely, it was not the decomposed corpse that heard and responded to the call of Jesus, but the dead man's soul—summoned from the other world to return to his body. Jesus will do the same thing at the general resurrection of the righteous and the wicked at the end of the age (John 5:28; 1Thess.4:14-18).

Fourth, Jesus taught that the soul survives the body. One such teaching is recorded in Luke 16:19-31. It is strongly suggested that you read this text from the Bible. It is not a parable but a true story.

Two men, one rich and lives luxuriously, but he lacks basic human compassion. He is called a certain man to protect his identity because he had family. The other man was a poor beggar named, Lazarus. He was left at the rich man's gate each day with the hope of being fed. But he was ignored by this heartless man.

In the process of time, they both died. The rich man was buried lavishly in keeping with his wealth and status. The poor man's body was either buried or discarded and burnt with the garbage as the custom was. But his soul was carried by angels into Paradise, *referred to as Abraham's bosom*. But that is not the end of the story.

Both men are shown conscious with their senses in a real place in the afterlife. The rich man in torment begging for water, but the poor man is comfortable in a place of bliss. They recognized each other but were in separate compartments with no crossing over. The rich man remembers that he had five brothers and wanted a message sent to them, but his request was denied. Bear in mind that these two men were very much alive outside of their bodies.

Fifth, Jesus demonstrated by His own death and resurrection that the life of the soul continues after physical death. Jesus was out of His body for three days while His body was in a tomb in Jerusalem. Just before the breath left His body, Jesus said to a repentant thief, "Today you will be with me in paradise (Luke 23:42-43). Jesus descended into hades or Paradise, somewhere in the underworld and he was not in the body (Eph.4:9; 1Peter 3:18-20).

The Apostles' Creed is the oldest of the many creeds of the Church; it captures the apostles' beliefs and practices. Speaking of the death of Jesus the creed says, "[He] suffered under Pontius Pilate, was crucified, died, and buried; He descended into hell. The third day He rose again from the dead..."[2]

Sixth, Jesus taught that there will be a resurrection for the righteous as well as a resurrection for the unrighteous. Both will be called back. In fact, they will hear the voice of the Lord and will come out of their graves (John 5:28). Souls will be reunited with their bodies as millions are called back to life.

Seven, the apostles continued the teachings of Jesus on the afterlife throughout the New Testament; it affirms there is an afterlife (1Cor. 15: 50-58; 1Thess. 4:16-18; Rev.20:11-15).

Being Absent from the Body

The Bible provides interesting insights in 2 Corinthians 5 about human beings in relation to their bodies. We look at five here.

First, the body is a place; it is called our earthly house or tent, our natural dwelling place (2 Cor.5:1).

Second, there is such a thing as being absent from our own body (vv.6-9). Being absent from the body is not the so-called near-death experience. Near-death is different from death; it does not fit the Christian biblical understanding of death. To be absent from the body is to be present somewhere else. In this case, with the Lord (v.6). When we are absent from this house, we have completely left the house and is present at another place.

Third, our earthly house can be destroyed or decomposed, but even so we do not cease to exist.

Fourth, God has an identical body for each of us, not made with human hands, an eternal house awaiting us in heaven (vv.1-2).

Five, a soul away from its body is considered naked, which means the body is our natural clothing. The righteousness of Christ is our spiritual clothing. The implication is that we are naked at death and will not be clothed until resurrection day when all will get their new bodies. This is one reason the dead cannot return, and if they return, we could not see them because the soul or spirit is invisible to the human eye. But they are very much alive and conscious where they are with the Lord.[3]

A soul being with the Lord does not necessarily mean that soul is in a happy place. With the Lord, therefore, means at a place exclusively under God's control. From our previous story of the rich man and Lazarus (Luke (16:19-31), we learned that both men are experiencing different conditions in the afterlife. This tells us wicked souls are in a place suitable to their eternal destination. The same is true of the souls of the righteous; they are experiencing bliss in keeping with their eternal destination.

Summary

Humans are both mortal and immortal in the secondary sense. The natural body dies but the soul or spirit lives on. Humans possess a soul or spirit that consciously survives the body. But only those humans with a salvation experience before physical death will enter heaven to enjoy eternal bliss with God.

Humans that die physically without a salvation experience with Jesus Christ will also live eternally but in a place of tormented separation from God. This is what the word perish in John 3:16 points.

CHAPTER 4

RESURRECTION OF THE BODY

Jesus the Guarantor

Jesus stands as the guarantor of life for all human resurrections. "As in Adam all die, even so in Christ shall all be made alive" (1Cor.15:22). All means all righteous persons and all unrighteous.

In chapter 1 we discussed the first half of this verse that speaks to the universality of sin and the universality of death. All humans have sinned, and all are under the sentence of death. Because of sin, we are all born spiritual dead and eventually we will all die physically. Just as there is a resurrection for spiritual death, there is a resurrection for physical death; in this chapter, it is labeled bodily resurrection. Later, it will be made clear why the word bodily is chosen over the word physical.

Bodily resurrection is what everybody looks forward to with eager anticipation; it gives hope and meaning to life. But history has only given us one such resurrection, and it is that of our Lord Jesus Christ, and He has guaranteed that all humans will be resurrected to life again but not at the same time nor for the same destination.

The Model Resurrection

The resurrection of Jesus Christ stands as the model for all end-time resurrections; it is unparallel and unique. There has never been another resurrection like it in all of history. God has promised to raise all humans after the resurrection model of His Son, to one degree or another (1Cor.15:22). They will not all be raised in the same order or have the same destination, but all will be raised.

You might be saying, what about those who were raised from the dead by prophets and apostles? Yes, in the Old Testament (OT), the prophet Elijah and others raised people from the dead, but they all died again. The same is true in New Testament (NT); Jesus and the apostles raised people from the dead, but they all died again.

Among those Jesus raised from the dead was His friend Lazarus who was dead and buried for four days (John 11:1-44). Well, like all the others, except Jesus, Lazarus died again. The resurrection of Jesus Christ is the first of its kind; He is in the firstfruits category.

Since the world began and humans live on it, Jesus Christ is the only one to have truly conquered dead. He died and was buried for three days and was raised from the dead and is alive today. His death and resurrection are clearly documented in History including the NT; all twenty-seven books bear witness to the resurrection of Jesus. There is no need to try to repeat the evidence here.

The Word of God says, Jesus died once and dies no more, that death has no more dominion over Him (Rom.6:9). He conquered death for all humankind and guarantees everyone a bodily resurrection in the time of the end. "For as in Adam all die, even so in Christ shall all be made alive" (1Cor.15:22).

Uniqueness of Christ's Resurrection Body

The Lord Jesus was unique in life, death, and resurrection; yet He was like us in every way except He was sinless (Heb.4:15). In life there was nothing striking about His appearance that set Him apart from other humans (Isa.53:1-3). The night of His arrest, Judas had to point Him out to the arresting party (Matt.26:47-50). In like manner, His resurrection body bears sameness to His pre-death body, yet it had significant functional differences.

Sameness—the following are examples of His sameness:

- The disciples recognized Him as the same person, and He recognized them just as before (Matt.28:9-10,16-20; John 21:1-14).
- His body bore the marks of His passion (Luke 24:39-41).
- He ate with His disciples as before (vv.42-43; John 21:4-14).
- The disciples touched Him, proving He was not a spirit (Luke 24:37-38).

Differences—the following are the differences:

- He controlled when to be recognized (Luke 24:13-32).
- He could appear and disappear at will (v.31; John 20:19-23).

- He could walk through closed doors (v.36; John 20:19-23, 26-29).
- His body dies no more (Rom.6:9-10; Rev.1:18).
- He is not restrained by gravity (Acts 1:9-11).

In as much as the resurrection of Christ is the model for human bodily resurrections, it does not mean that each human body rising from the dead will be a carbon copy of Christ's resurrection body. Frankly, all will be alike to one degree or another, but no one will be exactly alike; each will continue to have their own personality.

Furthermore, while all humans are guaranteed resurrection, they will not all have exactly the same body. Believers will be given a resurrection body closer to that of Christ resurrection body. The Bible states that God will fashion the believers' body like unto his glorious body (Phil.3:21), while unbelievers will be given a body to suit their eternal destination (Rev.20:11-15). We will return to this issue in chapters 4 and 5.

Christ the Firstfruits

The resurrection of Christ is classified the firstfruits from among the dead. This means there is a guaranteed greater harvest to follow, a quantitively greater resurrection of all humankind. The apostle Paul expresses it this way:

> But now is Christ risen from the dead, and has become the firstfruits of those who have fallen asleep. For since by man came death, by Man also came the resurrection of the dead. For as in Adam all die, even so in Christ all shall be made alive. But

each one in his own order: Christ the firstfruits, afterward those who are Christ's at His coming. 1Cor.15:20-23 NKJV)

The expression, *firstfruits,* is an agricultural term, one of the seven feasts of God established by law in ancient Israel (Lev.23:9-14). It marks the beginning of the harvest season as the first ripe fruits begin to come in. The firstfruits belong to God, and the farmers were required by law to bring the firstfruits to the priest at the house of God. By doing that, God guaranteed the greater harvest to follow. Neither natural disaster, disease, marauding thieves, vandals, wild animals, or anything else would preempt a successful harvest because God upholds His end of the agreement.

Firstfruits has a symbolic meaning also; it points to the resurrection of the Christ as the first one to rise from among the dead. His resurrection guarantees the greater resurrection of all humankind to follow. As sure as God raised Jesus from the dead, He will raise all Humankind at the time appointed. "For as in Adam all die, even so in Christ shall all be made alive" (1 Cor.15:22).

But take note of verse twenty-three. It says, "But each one in his own order: Christ the firstfruits, afterward those that are of Christ at His coming" (v.23 NKJV). It beckons us for more explanation.

Resurrection Order

The preceding verse twenty-three is clearly affirming that all humankind will be resurrected indeed, but not all at the same time; there is a divine order established by God. What is that general order? Christ first, believers second, unbelievers last.

Jesus Christ is already risen from the dead; He is the firstfruits of them that slept, first from among the dead. Then they that are of Christ, that is believers, will be resurrected when the Lord Jesus comes calling for them from the atmospheric heaven (1Thes.4:16-18). Unbelievers will be resurrected after Christ returns to earth, but at the very end of the millennium (Rev.20:11-15).

We know from other scripture passages that unbelievers are not of Christ, but they too will be resurrected sometime after the second coming of the Christ (John 5:28). For this reason, the focus of the next two chapters is the believers' resurrection, and the unbelievers' resurrection.

The Bible teaches that the resurrection of the dead is a lastdays event. The last days is a period from the resurrection of Jesus Christ to His Second Coming. Peter refers to it at the outpouring of the Holy Spirit on the Day of Pentecost, fifty-days after the resurrection of Christ as a last-days even (Acts 2:14-21).

So, we in the 21st century are living in the last days for two thousand years now. The preaching of the gospel is a last-days event. You may say two thousand years is a long time; no, it is not! With God it is just two days (2 Peter 3 3-10).

The point of emphasis is this—the resurrection of Christ has already taken place, believers, and unbelievers are waiting for theirs. The gospel message is to get people ready as to which group of resurrected folks they want to be in. All resurrected folks do not have the same destination. That is determined by their relationship with Jesus Christ.

It is the preached gospel and the blessed Holy Spirit that bring unbelievers into a believing, saving relationship with Jesus Christ (Matt.1:21;Acts2:36-41;Rom.10:9-15). This relationship with Jesus

Christ is spoken of as being born again into the kingdom of God, a spiritual birth from above (John 3:1-8).

Summary

Christ arose from the dead bodily; He returned to heaven bodily, and He will return to earth bodily (Acts 1:9-11; 1Thes.4:16-18).

Jesus was seen by witnesses innumerable after His resurrection, few fellowshipped with Him, and some ate with Him (John 21: 1-25; 1Cor.15:17).

The word of God makes it clear that all humankind will be raised from the dead bodily, and all will face judgment in the body for the deeds done in the body (John 5:28; 2 Cor.5:10).

Each person will return as he or she was, in the sense of personality identification. No one will return as something else or someone else. You are going to be you! Christ is the model; He came back bodily and so will you.

The Bible does not teach reincarnation (an Eastern philosophy); it teaches resurrection of the dead according to the order determined by God Himself (1Cor.15:23).

"Unless a grain of wheat falls into the ground and dies, it remains alone; but if it dies, it produces much grain" (John 12:23 NKV).

CHAPTER 5

BELIEVERS' RESURRECTION

Who Is a Believer?

We do not have the space in this short book to beat around the bush, so here is the short answer. A believer is a person who in faith responds positively to the gospel message of Jesus Christ, and that response results in a born-again experience. He or she is baptized in water and is received into the fellowship of believers or church (John 3: 1-18; Acts 2:36-41).

Can a person fake being saved? Yes, but he will not be fooling anyone else but himself. Acts 8 (9-24) is a good example of a faker. Here we find the story of a sorcerer who was baptized in water and was received into the fellowship of the local church, but his life was not truly changed. The Holy Spirit empowered apostles exposed his hypocrisy. The faker turned out to be the loser and the foolish one in the story.

As stated in chapter 1 of this book, the born-again experience is considered a spiritual resurrection (Eph.2:1-2). The soul or spirit is awakened, and the person is united to Christ. There is no substitute for a born-again experience. Good works, joining a church without repentance, getting baptized without repentance will not do. A born-again person is a changed person (2 Cor.5:17).

The Resurrection of Life

The believers' bodily resurrection is also called, "the resurrection of life." Here are the words of Jesus:

> Do not be amazed at this, for a time is coming when all who are in their graves will hear his voice and come out—those who have done what is good will rise to live, and those who have done what is evil will rise to be condemned. (John 5:28-29)

There are two resurrections spoken of in the preceding quotation: the resurrection of life, and the resurrection of condemnation. One is for believers, and the other for unbelievers. Our focus here is on the one for believers, the resurrection of life. It will take place a great while before the second, at least a thousand years (Rev.20:4-6).

The resurrection of life includes the righteous of all time periods or ages, which includes both Old Testament (OT) and New Testament (NT) believers, plus martyrs of the *Great Tribulation*. So, there are at least three sub-groups in the resurrection of life. We will briefly consider them here.

Group #1: This is believed to be the largest group; it includes all OT and NT believers. They are resurrected in what is commonly referred to as the rapture (1Thess.4:16-18). Living believers will also be transformed and raptured at this time (1Cor.15:51-58).

There are Bible scholars that teach otherwise—they believe and teach that NT believers who constitute the Church Age will not be resurrected the same time with OT believers, among them J. Dwight Pentecost (1958, 395-407).[1] This author among other Bible teachers do not agree with their position. Why?

There are several reasons we believe that NT and OT believers will all be resurrected at the same time, two are given here. (1) Both OT and NT believers are redeemed the same way—through the sacrifice Christ offered to God on the cross (Isa.53; John 1:29). OT believers were looking forward to the cross, while NT believers look back at the same cross (Acts.4:12). (2) Jesus said there would be one sheep and one shepherd (John 10:11-16; Eph.2:11-22).

Group#2 consists of believers that come through, at least, the first half of the *Great Tribulation*. They did not make it in the rapture because they were not born-again when the rapture took place. Many of them are church members and preachers and know enough Bible not to take the mark of the beast or worship his image. By embracing Christ and resisting taking the mark of the beast they are killed, millions of them worldwide. These believers are resurrected to join Group #1 in heaven (Rev.7:9-10). Bible teachers refer to them as tribulation saint or martyrs. But they should not be confused with Group 3.

Group#3 is consisted of martyrs killed by the antichrist late in the seven years of Great Tribulation. We know that because they are not resurrected until Christ returns to earth with Groups #1 & 2 that were earlier taken to heaven. Believers are seen in heaven in Revelation (7:9-10) and 19:1-10). Christ returns to earth with all believers in Revelation 19:11-16. Group 3 believer are resurrected in Revelation 20:4-6; that is after Christ returns to earth.

All three groups of believers together constitute the "first resurrection"(Rev.20:6). Why? Because they are the first group of humans from among the dead, and they are all believers. They came to Christ at different time and under different circumstances, but they are believers. They form a resurrection category unto themselves (see Vol.1 *The Rapture*, pp.52-56).[2]

This glorious outcome for believers is made possible because of the sacrifice of Christ on the cross, followed by His triumphant resurrection as the firstfruits from among the dead. Through Christ, believers have conquered the three stages of death. The second death (i.e., eternal death) will have no power over them (Rev.20: 6). All three groups of believers possess eternal life, which is not only longevity of life but life in its growing fullness of quality.

The thing to remember is the fact that all humans will not be resurrected at the same time; there is a resurrection order and category: Christ the firstfruits, then believers, then unbelievers.

Believers' Resurrection Body

We do not have comprehensive knowledge about the believers' resurrection body, but the Scripture provides a significant amount of information, some of which we will try to capture in this section. Certain information is partly classified, not yet revealed.

First, believers' resurrection body will be like the resurrection body of our Lord Jesus Christ. The apostle John writes, "Beloved, now we are the children of God; and it has not yet been revealed what we shall be, but we know that when He is revealed, we shall be like Him, for we shall see Him as He is..."(1 John 3:2). The full information is partly classified (hidden) and partly revealed.

Second, if we are going to be like the resurrected Christ, as stated, then His resurrection body provides clues (see chapter 4, the section, Uniqueness of Christ's body). His resurrected body dies no more, ours will die no more. He was not a spirit, He was real, ours will be real as well. Christ's resurrection body was not restricted by gravity, so will that of believers.

Third, the resurrection body is a spiritual body (1Cor.15:44-46). Note that I did not say, a spirit body but a spiritual body. A spirit is ghostly, you cannot touch or hold it; it cannot eat food. The resurrection body of Jesus Christ is a spiritual body; that is the kind of body believers will have when they are resurrected or transformed. What is so different about a spiritual body?

The life principle of a spiritual body is not blood but the spirit. The life principle of the physical body is in the blook, so it is subject to corruption, death, and decay. That is why flesh and blood cannot inherit the kingdom of God; blood has a short shelf life, spirit is eternal. Post-resurrection—Jesus said to His disciples, "Look at my hands and feet. It is I myself! Touch me and see, a ghost does not have flesh and bone as you see me have" (Luke 24: 36-39).

The resurrected body is not composed of dust like our current physical body; it is made in heaven from classified components and can live comfortably anywhere in the universe. How do we know this? Here is an intelligence report from the Word of God on the believers' new body from heaven:

> For we know that if the earthly tent we live in is destroyed, we have a building from God, an eternal

> house in heaven, not build by human hands. Meanwhile we groan, longing to be clothed instead with our heavenly dwelling, because when we are clothed, we will not be found naked. For while we are in this tent, we groan and are burdened, because we do not wish to be unclothed but to be clothed instead with our heavenly dwelling, so that what is mortal may be swallowed up by life. Now the one who has fashioned us for this very purpose is God, who has given us the Spirit, guaranteeing what is to come.
>
> Therefore, we are always confident and know that as long as we are at home in the body, we are away from the Lord...I would prefer to be away from the body and at home with the Lord.... (2 Cor.5:1-6)

The preceding quote is self-explanatory with many insights on the believers' new resurrection body. At death we step out of our earthly body, and perhaps, we remain unclothed until the time of resurrection when we are fitted with our new body from heaven. We have borne the image of the earth man (i.e., Adam) and we will bear the image of the heavenly (i.e., Christ) (1 Cor.15:47-49).

Fourth, the resurrection body is powerful and glorious (1Cor.15: 42). When the physical body dies it has no power; it is buried in weakness, but it will be raised in power (v.42). The resurrection of Christ illustrates this point for it was raised with great power.

Matthew explains—he speaks of Christ's resurrection in the context of descending angels, earthquake so powerful, hardened, burly, Roman soldiers were knocked off their feet and fell to the ground as dead men (Matt.28:1-4). When they regained their composure, they ran from the scene like scared rabbits to report to their superiors what had happened (vv.11-15).

Fifth, the resurrection body dies no more; it is not subject to corruption, decay, and death; it is immortal (1Cor.15:50-54). It is raised a glorious body (v.43). Glorious in this context means without defects, pristine, beautiful, bright, with full potential. The apostle Paul reminds us that our Lord Jesus will "transform our lowly body that it may be conformed to His glorious body…" (Philip.3:20-21).

The Holy Spirit's Resurrection Role

Despite the assertion made by Jesus that no person takes His life from Him, that He had power to lay it down and power to pick it up again (John 10:17-18), His resurrection was the activity of the Holy Trinity: Father, the Son, and Holy Spirit. Each personality played a significant role in the bodily resurrection of Jesus.

But the role of the Holy Spirit is somewhat shrouded, especially when preached in contemporary churches. In this section, the role of the Holy Spirit is highlighted because His presence in the life and ministry of Christ reveals comparative insights as to how the Holy Spirit works in the life of believers. We will compare three areas of Christ's life with that of the believers.

First, we look at Mary's conception and birth of Jesus. A review of the narrative reveals the involvement of God the Father, angels, the Holy Spirit, and humans. God the Father sent a messenger, the angel Gabriel, to a Virgin named Mary, engaged to be married to a man named Joseph (Luke1:26-30).

The message of the angel to Mary was, "You will conceive and give birth to a son, and you will name him Jesus. He will be great and will be called the Son of the Most High. The Lord God will give him the throne of his father David, and he will reign over Jacob's descendants forever; his kingdom will have no end" (vv31-33).

Mary being a virgin, and not ignorant of human reproductive biology, asked the angel, "How will this be...since I am a virgin?" (v.34). The angel responded, "The Holy Spirit will come upon you, and the power of the Most High will overshadow you. So, the holy one to be born will be called the Son of God" (v.35). The explanation of the angel being satisfactory to Mary, she gave her consent (v.38).

The Holy Spirit was very active and involved in the life of Jesus and in the lives of those closely associated with His birth. Mary's cousin Elizabeth, six months pregnant with John the Baptist was, perhaps, the first to receive the revelation of Mary's pregnancy, and the Holy Spirit was the agent of that revelation; she was filled with Holy Spirit in the process (vv.39-45). Mary, inspired by the blessed Holy Spirit prophesied and worshipped (vv.46-55).

Now, notice the parallel comparison with Jesus and believers. Believers enter the kingdom of God through a spiritual birth and the Holy Spirit is the agent of that birth (John 3:1-8). David Pawson asserts that "the Holy Spirit is the obstetrician" that presides over the believers' birth into the kingdom of God.[3]

Second, the Holy Spirit empowered the life and ministry of Jesus. Jesus was baptized by the Holy Spirit at the time of His water baptism in the Jordan River. This was the inauguration of Jesus' public ministry (Matt.3:16-17, 4:1). He was subsequently tested by Satan and won the victory through the power of the Holy Spirit, fasting and prayer, and the power of the Word of God (Luke 4:1-13).

Jesus started and ended His ministry work under the anointing and power of the Holy Spirit (vv.14-21). Peter witnessing to

Cornelius and those at his house said, "...God anointed Jesus of Nazareth with the Holy Spirit and power, and how he went around doing good and healing all who were under the power of the devil....They killed him by hanging him on a cross, but God raised him from the dead on the third day and caused him to be seen..."(Acts 10: 37-40).

Observe the comparison. Just as the Holy Spirit anointed and empowered the life and ministry of Jesus, so the Holy Spirit anoints and empowers believers to live victorious lives, and to service effectively in the work of the ministry (Acts 1:4-8). The Holy Spirit empowered not only the Jerusalem people group, who were mostly Jews gathered on the Day of Pentecost (Acts 2:1-48). But He anointed and empowered Samaritans (Acts 8:11-23), Gentiles at Caesarea (Acts 10:44-48, Greeks at Antioch (11:19-26, 13:1-3), and to the Ephesians as well (Acts 19:1-5). What is the lesson?

The clear answer to the question is this—the model of the Holy Spirit upon the life and ministry of Jesus Christ is the model for all believers in Christ and in the ministry (Acts 2:38-39).

Third, the Holy Spirit's involvement in the resurrection and ascension of our Lord Jesus Christ. There are numerous Scripture passages affirming that God raised Jesus from the dead (e.g., Acts 2:22-36, 4:8-10, 13:30-36). But note also that the power of the Holy Spirit raised Jesus from the dead and the same Holy Spirit indwells believers and will raise them from the dead in the resurrection of the righteous (Rom.1:1-4,8:10-11). Jesus Himself is the resurrection and the life (John 11:25-26). What is the lesson here?

Just as the Holy Spirit participated in the resurrection of Jesus Christ, He will raise believers from the dead to a bodily resurrection like our Lord's (Rom.8:10-11; 1 John 3: 2-3). When we first come to

Christ, a resurrection from spiritual death takes place through the agency of the Holy Spirit (Eph.2:1-6). This is the same as being born again into the kingdom of God by an act of the Spirit. In other words, spiritual resurrection and the new birth are the same and they are done through the agency of the Holy Spirit (John 3:1- 21).

The Mystery of the Resurrection

When the Bible speaks of mystery, it generally means knowledge that is unrevealed; the information is with God, but it is classified. It is not yet made known to humans in full; the believers' resurrection body falls in this category of classification. Some elements are revealed and come are classified.

For this reason, the apostle John speaking of the believers' future states, "Beloved, now we are children of God; and it has not yet been revealed what we shall be, but we know that when He is revealed, we shall be like Him, for we will see Him as He is" (1John 3:2 NKJV). John is not the only one to make this assertion.

The apostle Paul also speaks of this mystery extensively and reveals tremendous insights, much of which we have already discussed. But we will now revisit his resurrection discourse in 1Corinthians 15 (NKJV) and glean insights we overlooked.

First, Paul asked the rhetorical question, "But some will say, 'How are the dead raise up? And with what body do they come?'" (v.35). To answer the question, he invites us to examine sprouting seeds in a vegetable garden. He says, "Foolish one, what you sow is not made alive unless it dies" (v.36). Before Paul, Jesus spoke of His death and resurrection using similar words, "...unless a grain of wheat falls into the ground and dies, it remains alone; but if it dies, it produces much grain" (John 12 24).

What Jesus and Paul show us is the first mystery of agriculture, the seed we put in the ground dies, we can see the husk of it, yet it lives. Back to Paul, "God gives it a body as He pleases, and to each seed its own body" (1 Cor.15:38). When we sow corn, why don't we get watermelons in return? because God determined from creation that each seed must produce after its kind (Gen.1:11-12). The same is true for animals and humans, they are all self-producing after their kind (vv.20-23, 27-28). That is the way God order things from the beginning and this Divine mystery baffles us all.

But what is the lesson Paul is teaching about the resurrection of humans with the agricultural illustration? There are many but we will consider two. (1) Like a seed that falls into the ground dies and yet lives, a human being dies and is buried. But will rise again, not as a cat, or dog, or some other animal, but as a human being. Just as corn retains its identity and does not become a watermelon, humans retain theirs as well; they do not become a lesser being like a dog, or a greater being like an angel. Resurrection is biblical, reincarnation is not.

(2) When a seed dies, it not only produces new life with the same body or identity, but it also multiplies. God gave one seed, His Son, and by reason of His death and resurrection, God has many children, sons and daughters.

Second, Paul describes the gloriousness of the resurrection body (1Cor.15:39-49 NKJV). He calls our attention to astronomy; look at the heavenly bodies, the sun, the moon, and stars, they are all glorious, but they differ in glory. The resurrection body will be glorious but differ in glory from the bodies of the planetary heaven.

Paul goes on to give us details about the gloriousness of the resurrection body by contrasting the indignities of death and dying that the body goes through with the glory of resurrection (vv.42-45). There is no glory in a dead body being disposed of. It is buried or disposed of as a perishable, decaying corpse, but it will be raised imperishable (v.43). It is buried or disposed of in dishonor but will be resurrected in glory (v.43). It is disposed of in weakness but is raised in power (v.43). It is buried as a natural body but resurrected as a spiritual body (v.44).

Since believers' resurrection body will be like the resurrection body of Jesus, we can contrast our death and resurrection with the His death and resurrection. If there is a dignified way of dying, Jesus' death by crucifixion was not one of them. He was beaten most brutally at His trial, weakened by it He fell under the weight of the cross and was helped by Simon of Cyrene. Jesus was stripped naked, and nailed to a wooden cross; they hung Him high to die, suffocating under the weight of His own body.

His body would have been taken down and disposed of at the city dump and burnt with the garbage. But two secret disciples, Joseph of Arimathea, and Nicodemus, spared Him that further indignity. They stepped forward, claimed the body, and gave Him a decent burial (John 19:38-42).

But now look again at the resurrection and the resurrection body of Jesus. The resurrection was so powerful, bright, and glorious that it blinded and knocked Roman soldiers off their feet (Matt.28:1-4, 11-15). He could withhold His identity, vanish at will, even walk through closed doors (Luke 24: 13-31,36-43; John20:19-20). The full glory of Christ resurrection body given by the apostle John in the book of Revelation (Rev.1:10-18).

But above all, note the concluding description of the risen, glorified Christ whom John saw, "... His countenance was like the sun shining in its strength. And when I saw Him, I fell at His feet as dead (vv.16-17). The Bible tells us that the believers' resurrection body will be fashioned lie unto the glorious body of Jesus Christ (Phil.3:20-21).

A Spiritual Body

One of the eye-opening things we learn from the apostle Paul is that the believers' body is buried as a natural body but is raised as a spiritual body. He emphasized the point by saying, "There is a natural body and there is a spiritual body" (1Cor.15:44).

We come to understand in our previous discussion that the *spiritual body* bears the identity of the *natural body*, but it has many functional differences such as being more powerful, more glorious, can walk through closed doors, and it can defy the laws of gravity as we see in the ascension of Jesus (Acts 1:9-11).

But above all, it is immortal, it dies no more. So, the resurrection transforms the natural body into a body that is immortal. And believers who will be alive when Jesus returns and for that reason will not experience the usual physical death, will go through a transformation process from mortal to immortality, which is the equivalent of physical death (1 Cor.15:50-58).

Summary

The believers' resurrection and resurrection body are significant aspects of the blessed hope in Jesus (Titus 2:11-14). Everything about the believers' present and future life rest on the resurrection of Jesus Christ. The whole Christian faith stands or falls with the resurrection of Jesus Christ (1 Cor.15:12-19).

In this chapter we defined a believer to be a person who has had a born-again experience, and is baptized in water, and is received into a local fellowship or church. The born-again or new birth experience is considered a spiritual resurrection (Eph.2:1).

We discussed the believers' resurrection and resurrection body, showing that it is patterned off the resurrection and resurrection body of Jesus Christ. As His body was powerful, glorious, and immortal so will the believers' resurrection body.

Just as the blessed Holy Spirit plays a significant role in Jesus' conception and birth, life and ministry, resurrection, and ascension, so the Holy Spirit plays a pivotal role in the believers' spiritual birth, spiritual life, and in their resurrection at the end of the age.

Not all that can be known about the believers' resurrection and resurrection body are known; both have elements of mystery or information that is classified or not yet revealed. Somethings we know in part but when the Lord comes the full revelation will be made known (1Cor.13:12).

CHAPTER 6

UNBELIEVERS' RESURRECTION

It is the Word of God that tells us who a believer is, and the same Word of God identifies who the unbelievers are. The Word of God is the constitution of God's kingdom and sets the requirement for entry into the kingdom. Humans cannot set their own standard for getting into heaven. That thinking or belief is absurd.

Because some humans insist on this absurdity, we end up with a broad road with many lanes of choice with people dancing their way to heaven as if they are going to meet the Wis of Oz. The problem is that none of those lanes lead to heaven. People like to say, there are many paths to the top of the mountain, but when we get there, we all have the same view. That may be true of a mountain but certainly not heaven or eternal life. There are entry requirements, but they are not determined by mere mortals.

Jesus has given us many instructive keys to better identify the path to His kingdom: Here is one: "Enter through the narrow gate. For wide is the gate and broad is the road that leads to destruction, and many enter through. But small is the gate and narrow the road that leads to life, and only a few find it" (Matt.6:13-14).

The small gate is not hidden; it is obvious to those who are thoughtfully looking for it. A small gate and a narrow road speak to a disciplined lifestyle free of excessive baggage; whereas the wide gate and the broad road are the very opposite, they speak of an undisciplined, unspiritual, and unbiblical lifestyle.

The King of the kingdom sets the terms for those who want to enter His kingdom; humans cannot set their own terms of entry. The Bible, God's Word, is the admissions manual; it lays out the terms of entry into the Kingdom of God. You must be a believer!

But who is a believer? This is where things get very tricky, because people are inclined to invent their own definitions; some say, it is a person who does a fair amount of good, kind, charitable, one who helps the community. Others say, it is a religious person; he is baptized, he goes to church, he is a good neighbor. The problem is this—a person can be all that and more, yet completely miss the kingdom of God and heaven. Here is what Jesus said:

> Not everyone who say to Me, Lord, Lord, shall enter the kingdom of heaven, but he who does the will of My Father in heaven. Many will say to Me on that day, Lord, Lord, have we not prophesied in Your name, cast out demons in Your name, and done many wonders in Your name? And then I will declare to them, I never knew you; depart from Me, you who practice lawlessness! (Matt.7:21-23).

It is evident that the "many people" in the quotation thought they were believers. They were church members, church leaders, preachers, pastors, and evangelists. They were all active in ministry prophesying, healing, working miracles, and casting out demons. In appearance and ministry outcome, they are model believers. But Jesus said, "depart from me…, I never knew you."

How could they be so wrong? What a disappointment! The best explanation is—they ignored the requirements of the admissions manual. They cast aside the Word of God, for the traditions of men, thinking their good works would gain them entrance into the kingdom of God. They sought admission on their own terms.

There are churches that operate like that; some are mega, some large, and some small. They throw the word of God aside; they do not preach repentance. They do not demand changed lives and holiness in living. They entertain all kinds of unbiblical lifestyles, and think they are on their way to heaven, but they are not.

The Bible said, they are on the broad road to destruction, not heaven (Luke 13:22-30). God will not justify what He cannot sanctify. Jesus saves people from their sins, not in their sins (Matt.1:21). He commands repentance to be preached in His name, and the disciples obeyed (Luke 24.45-49; Acts 2 33-41).

We ask the question again, who is a believer? Here is the biblical answer. A believer is a person with a saving relationship with Jesus Christ; the person is born again into the kingdom (John 3:1-21).

Let us look carefully through these 21 verses to make clear who unbelievers are. We will go to-and-fro between believer and unbeliever, because if you know one you will know the other. The general key in the definition is a relationship with Jesus Christ. You must authentically know Jesus, and He must know you. But now note the main issues Jesus reveals in the text (John 3:-21):

- It is beyond being good or religious, Nicodemus was all that and more; it is being born again into the kingdom (vv.1-5).
- It is experiencing a spiritual birth from above through the agency of the Holy Spirit; it is as mysterious as the wind, supernatural, and heavenly (vv.6-14).
- It is a faith experience that gives you eternal life now through a saving relationship with Jesus Christ (vv.15-18).
- It is an experience of coming out of darkness to light and moving from falsehood to truth (vv.19-21).

The unbeliever is the person who has not experienced all the preceding, he is not born again, he has no saving relationship with Jesus Christ, he abides in darkness and does not know the truth. He remains in spiritual death, yet alive physically (Eph.2:1-3).

There are certain types of sins that head the list as being deprave, repulsive, and abominable to God, and people who practice them in church or out of church will not inherit the kingdom of God (Rom.1:18-23; 1Cor.6:9-11). Rather than repent, people tend to say, they were born that way. But whether they were born that way, socialized that way or chose to be that way, the Word of God calls them to repentance. That means a radical change. Nobody gets a pass to get into heaven without repenting, confessing, and forsaking their sins.

We were all born sinners, and God demands change in all of us to enter His kingdom. God does not excuse any sin. He provides sufficient grace to deliver all of us from enslavement. We are commanded to present our bodies a living sacrifice, holy and acceptable to God, not conformed to this world system but transformed by the renewing of our minds that we may prove what the perfect will of God is (Rom.12:1-2).

Abiding in Spiritual Death

If the unbeliever does not experience the spiritual transformation spoken of in the previous section, he or she abides in a state of spiritual death and is under the wrath of God (John 3: 18-19).

To emphasize, when the unbeliever receives salvation from sin by coming to Jesus Christ in faith, he or she is born again and has crossed over from death to life, eternal life. Jesus said it this way, "Most assuredly, I say to you, he who hears My word and believes in Him who sent Me has everlasting life, and shall not come into judgment, but has passed from death to life" (John 5:24).

But if the unbeliever has not crossed over, he abides in the state of spiritual death under the wrath of God. This state of death is deceiving, because the dead does not know he is dead because he is alive naturally or physically and might be flourishing materially.

In other words, because of His common grace, God sends rain upon the just and the unjust. For this reason, it may not appear as if the unbeliever is under God's wrath. The goodness of God should lead a person to repentance but in most cases, unbelievers do not think that way. They are more inclined to credit their success to their own genius, instead of to the goodness of God.

Furthermore, some wealth are given by Satan (Matt.4:8-10). But Satan's goal is to "steal, kill, and destroy" that person in his time (John 10:10a KJV). So, material prosperity is no indication that the person is not spiritually dead and under God's wrath.

Therefore, it is important to understand this state of spiritual death because it is deceptive and can give a false sense of security. By this world's standard, life could be good for the spiritually dead person. This person could have a beautiful family, lives in a multimillion-dollar mansion, a billionaire with private jets, second and third homes and offices in New York, London, and Rome. Yet all he is in the sight of God is a poor, rich fool, the kind the Bible often speak about, rich in material things but poor toward God, poor in soul, and poor in things spiritual (Luke 12:16-21; 16:19-30).

If the unbeliever continues in this state of spiritual death until physical death comes to him or her, then that state of spiritual death transitions into the permanent state of eternal death.

The Path to Eternal Death

Eternal death is addressed in Chapter 1 but for the sake of clarity and convenience, we revisit it here. The Bible speaks of three levels of death: spiritual, physical, and eternal.

The simple definition of death is "separation." In spiritual death the person's soul or spirit is separated from God; it has no spiritual life (Eph.2:1). The person is more dead to God and to things spiritual than a deaf person to sound or a blind person to light.

Physical death is the separation of the soul or spirit from the physical body. Whereas eternal death is the permanent, eternal separation of the whole person (body, soul, spirit) from God in a confined and unpleasant environment (Luke 12:19-31).

Eternal death is the permanent state of separation of the whole person, body, soul, and spirit in hell eternally (Matt.10:28). Eternal death is also referred to as the second death (Rev.19:6). Or to be thrown into hell, the lake of burning sulfur(20:11-15. It is the unbelievers' end state, the opposite of eternal life that believers in Christ inherit. Eternal death in the lake of fire is what the words "shall not perish" warn us against in John 3:16.

The Resurrection of Damnation

The resurrection of believers is called the resurrection of life, whereas that of the unbelievers' is called, the resurrection of damnation (John 5:28). They do not take place at the same time; there is a resurrection order (1Cor.15:20-23).

The righteous will be resurrected at the rapture (1Thess.4:15-18), another group during the great tribulation (Rev.7:9-14), and another group when Christ returns at the end of the tribulation (Rev.20: 4-5). Both resurrections are separated by a thousand years.

Unbelievers are resurrected for the white throne judgment at the end of the millennium(Rev.20:11-15). Remember, the duration of the millennium is a thousand years. Unbelievers are lost! God has made it clear throughout the entire Bible that those who refuse His offer of salvation in Christ will perish (John 3:16).

The unbelievers' resurrection is the final resurrection. This resurrection will take place for three fundamental reasons. (1) It will take place to fulfill the prophetic text of Scripture. The Word of God states emphatically, "As in Adam all die, even so in Christ shall all be made alive"(1Cor.15:23).

(2) Unbelievers will be resurrected to face judgment for their sins (Heb.9:27-28). Believers will be resurrected to face judgment as well but for their works, not for their sins (2 Cor.5:10). Believers will face judgment but not condemnation (Rom.8:1-2, 31-39).

(3) Unbelievers will be resurrected to be judged and face the consequences of justice for their sins (Rev.20:11-15).

Summary

We have identified the unbeliever as a distinct group of people from believers. Believers are in Christ; they have accepted God's offer of salvation and eternal life through Jesus Christ. For that reason, they have passed from death to life, eternal life, and that is their lot.

Unbelievers have rejected God's offer of salvation. And for that reason, they abide in a state of spiritual death. If they continue in that state of death until they die physically, they are forever lost, because there is no repentance in the grave.

Unbelievers will be resurrected to face judgment for their sins, as well as the consequences. They will receive the opposite to eternal life; they will receive eternal death (Rev.20:11-15).

God is exceedingly generous. He gave His Son as a ransom, a substitutionary sacrifice and atonement for our sins (Isa.53, John 3:16). Some humans will accept God offer and be saved, but others will not; they will exercise their rights, reject the offer, and face the consequences for their sins.

He is no fool who accepts God offer of salvation. Everybody knows that if you reject the offer of life, you choose death by default (Rom.6:23). God respects our rights to choose our own destiny though He strongly warns us against it (John 3:14-18).

CHAPTER 7
ETERNAL LIFE

What is Eternal Life?

Throughout this book, we keep referring to the biblical term *eternal life* numerous times, but what does it mean, what does it contain? This chapter attempts to answer this question by exploring Christian understanding of the term as it is used in Scripture, most frequently by Jesus and the apostles. We will begin to answer the question by showing what *eternal life* is not.

First, eternal life is not mere longevity of life, so it "should not be confused with mere endless existence."[1] All humans possess endless existence with other spirit beings, like angels. Humans and angels and all other created life forms above the plant kingdom are creatures. Humans are both mortals and spirit beings because the body dies but the soul or spirit lives on (Ecc.12:1-7).

But humans are not angels, and they never will be; they are creatures below the angels (Psalm 8:4-8). Resurrected humans will be like angels, only in the sense that they will not marry or procreate (Matt.22:23-30). Created lower than the angels, does not mean inferior to the angels; humans are just different (Heb.2:5-12).

Jesus was not created but, in the incarnation, He was made lower than the angels, because He took on the image of humans, not angels. For that reason, He is brother to us, a status never accorded to angels (vv.10-11).

Second, we should not confuse eternal life with natural life. Natural life is subject to tremendous limitations such as susceptibility to disease, sickness, and death. We are also subject to certain environmental limitations. We were not created to live under water, fly unaided through the heavens, or live in outer space. Earth is the domain for which we were created.

Third, except for Adam, the first man, natural human life comes from human generation or procreation (Gen.1: 27-28; John 3: 6). The Creator of life arranged that everything should reproduce after its kind. We can prove this by experience and observation. We can hypothesize about being evolved from a lower form of life, but we can neither experience it nor prove it by observation in real time.

On the positive side, the first thing to consider is this--eternal life is so extensive that an exhaustive answer cannot be given for two reasons: 1) we can only speak of what is revealed in scripture, so where the scripture is silent, it is best that we be silent as well. Anything beyond that is mere speculation. 2) Much of what is to be known about eternal life remains classified in the kingdom of God. How do we know that?

The word of God explains for us. The apostle John informs us that "now we are the children of God, and what we will [become] has not yet been made know. But we know that when Christ appears, we shall be like, for we shall see him as he is" (1John 3:2). John is saying, our eternal life status is only partly known.

The other apostles used similar language. For example, the apostle Paul in 1Corinthians 3 says, "we declare God's wisdom, a mystery that has been hidden.... What no eye has seen, what no ear has heard, and what no human mind has conceived—the things God has prepared for those who love him—these are the things God has revealed by his Spirit" (vv.7-10). In other word, God's revelation is progressive, His revelation to humans is on a need-to-know basis. Revelation knowledge is always timely and useful.

There are things we humans want to know only out of sheer curiosity, but having knowledge of them now will not help us to live more godly, productive, and meaningful lives.

Furthermore, somethings God has prepared for His children are so intense, our natural, earthly body is not equipped to deal with them. For example, in the transfiguration experience, Jesus temporarily entered His glory to accommodate Moses and Elijah who appeared in glory. Peter, James, and John who were just in their natural bodies were overwhelmed, knocked off their feet and out of their senses for a while (Matt.17:1-8). How could they relate this other world story to make sense? Jesus told them to keep quiet until He is raised from the dead (v.9).

His resurrection would provide the context for others to understand the transfiguration phenomenon. The resurrection of the Christ was not only the breaking in of the new age (i.e., the last days), it was physically overwhelming experience to those that witnessed it. The soldiers guarding the tomb were knocked off there and feet to the ground like dead men (Matt.28:1-4). When they regained their composure, they fled the scene (vv. 11-15).

Another example. When the apostle John on the Isle of Patmos in the Aegean Sea, faced the full glory of the resurrected Christ, John was clearly knocked off his feet to the ground as a dead man (Rev. 1: 17-20). His natural body could not stand up to the intensity of the fully glorified Christ.

Second, eternal life is life in its fullness from a qualitative perspective. Humans reach their full potential for which they were created and subsequently redeemed. Jesus said, He came that we might have life and have it to the full (John 10:10b). It is evident that by fullness of life, He means the same as eternal life, not the end point but the beginning point because there is no end point (3:14-18). Eternal life, therefore, has unending growth possibilities.

Third, eternal life is life lived without lack, disease, or the possibility of death, because death itself will be done away with (1Cor.15:50-57; Rev.20: 13-15). The former things are passed away such as weeping, mourning, and death (Rev.22:4).

Fourth, eternal life is life lived in endless communion and fellowship in the immediate presence of God (Rev.22:3).

Fifth, eternal life is life lived in a completely new environment: new heaven, new earth, new everything (Rev.22:5).

Sixth, eternal life begins not when we die or when we are resurrected at the end of the age; it begins the moment we receive Jesus Christ as our Savior and Lord and are born again into the kingdom of God (John 3:1-21). In this reference, eternal life is stated and implied numerous times, and every time it has to do with a person's saving relationship with Jesus Christ.

Seven, eternal life is a priceless treasure, the gift of God (John 3:14-16; Rom.6:23). But there are people, like the rich young ruler of Mark (10:17-23) who desperately want eternal life but will walk away from Jesus, thinking discipleship with Him is too demanding.

We must remind them that eternal life is resident in Jesus Christ, to walk away from Him is to walk away from eternal life (John 3:16; Rom.6:23). Salvation from sin is found in no other name or person (Matt.1:21; Acts 4:12). Jesus, the Lamb of God is the only sacrifice for sin (Heb.6: 4-6).

Eternal Life—The Believers Inheritance

In my work, *The Book of Life & The Books of Wrath*, eternal life is classified as part of the believers' inheritance package.[2] You will notice that I said, "inheritance," not rewards. There is a notable difference in Scripture between these two categories, and this difference is reflected in my writing, especially this series (see Vol.2,*The Believers Judgment & Rewards*).

Rewards are given for work done for the kingdom of God out of love and obedience to Christ, for abuse endured for the Lord Jesus Christ in the line of duty, and for faithful, exemplary lives lived under unspeakable pressure (Matt.5:10-12,6:1-6; 1Cor.3:10-15; 2 Cor.5:10). A person cannot work his way into the kingdom of God, but once he is in the kingdom, he serves Christ out of love and receives a reward (1 Tim.4:5-8). Salvation is the gift of God (Rom.6: 23; Eph.2: 8). A gift is costly to the giver, but free to the receiver.

Inheritance is a gift bestowed based upon family relationship with God and His Son (Rom.8:14-17; Gal.4:4-7). Your paycheck is not a gift from your employer. It is a reward for work done. You earned it! You would be insane to quarrel with your employer with whom you have no blood relations for not naming you in his last will and testament. You can only quarrel legitimately if you have a filial relationship with the employer. A reward is earned, but an inheritance is gifted based on family relationship.

The Lord invites us to work in His vineyard and promises to pay us at the end of the day, but there is one caveat. We must not do it for self-glory for that would serve as our reward.

In other words, a believer can lose his or her reward in heaven because the work rendered in Christ's name was not done out of love and obedience to Christ (1Cor.3:6-15). People who do ministry for the glory of self, have no reward to receive in heaven (Matt.6:1-8). But those same people will not lose their inheritance (Eph.1:11-15; Col.1:12-14; 1Pet.1:3-5). Why?

Because going to heaven is not a reward given for good works done; it is the natural outcome of salvation (John 3:16). Our eternal inheritance is based upon our relationship with Jesus Christ.

Eternal life is the gateway gift in the believers' inheritance package; it is pivotal because all other gifts in the package hinges on it. For this reason, eternal life is the first gift to be received and it is received the very moment a person receives Jesus Christ as Savior and Lord.[3] Eternal life is resident in Jesus Christ, without Him the whole package is lost (John 3:14-18).

People who refuse eternal life while they are alive in the physical body are eternally lost. The wages or penalty for sin is death (Rom.6:23a). In this case eternal death or separation from God in hell (Rev.20: 11-15). Believers receive eternal life because they accept God's offer of salvation from sin through Jesus Christ. Unbelievers receive eternal death because they reject God's offer of salvation. By rejecting God's offer they are saying, we will pay our own way. Jesus is the only safe way (John 14:5-7).

The Purpose of Human Resurrection

This is the concluding section of this book, so let us bring back the resurrection of humans in focus. We stated on the scriptural premise that "as in Adam all die, so in Christ all will be made alive" (1Cor.15:22). In this one verse is the universality of death and the university of resurrection.

We have pointed out two major resurrection categories; they are the resurrection of the righteous, and the resurrection of the unrighteous. The apostle John refers to them as the resurrection of life, and the resurrection of damnation (John 5:28).

These two resurrections will not happen at the same time, nor for the same purpose, and the people in them will not be heading for the same destination. But why bring humans back to life? The answer could be extensive, but we will summarize it in three points.

First, physical death does not mean, the person is forever removed from existence and cease to live. They are merely separated from the physical body but very much alive somewhere.

Second, because God is holy, just, and true, He must hold every human responsible for their behavior, and He must call them to account. The Day of Judgment is that day of reckoning.

Third, because God is faithful and true, He must fulfill every promise made to humans. His word cannot and will not fall to the ground (Isa.55:8-11). The righteous is promised eternal life, which constitutes a package of many things: things revealed, and things yet to be revealed. God must make good on His promise to the righteous. God must also make good on His promise to the unrighteous or unbeliever. Like everybody else, God must hold them accountable, and they must be given their just due.

Volumes 9 and 10 in this series will provide more details on the eternal status of these two groups of humans; their status will be markedly different. Nobody should be surprised that this is so because the Word of God has consistently made this clear from Genesis to Revelation. The Word of God is not suggestions to be ignored; they are executive orders to be carried out or obeyed.

REFERENCES

Chapter 1 Understanding Sin and Death

1. Green, Bradley G. *The Gospel of the Mind, Recovering and Shaping the Intellectual Life.* Wheaton, IL: Crossway, 2010.

2. Unger, Merrill F. *The New Unger's Bible Dictionary.* R.K. Harrison, editor. Chicago, IL: Moody Bible Institute, 1988, 397

Chapter 3 Immortality of the Soul

1. The New Unger's Bible Dictionary, "*Immortality*"(609-611).

2. Holcomb, Justin S. *Know the Creeds and Councils.* Grand Rapids, MI: Zondervan, 2014.

3. Berkhof, Louis. *Systematic Theology, New Combined Edition.* Grand Rapids, MI: William B. Eerdmans Publishing Co.1996. 672-678.

Chapter 5 Believers' Resurrection

1. Pentecost, J. Dwight. *Things to Come, A Study in Biblical Eschatology*. Grand Rapids, MI: Zondervan, 1958. 395-407.

2. Dewar, Michael. *The Rapture*. Vol.1. Brooklyn, New York: Dwelling Place Cleansing, 2023. 52-56

3. Pawson, David, *The Normal Christian Birth: How to Give New Believers a Proper Start in Life.* London: Hodder & Stoughton, 1097.

Chapter 7 Eternal Life

1. *The New Unger's Dictionary* (Eternal life).

2. Dewar, Michael. *The Book of Life & The Books of Wrath*. Lake Mary, FL: Xulon Press, 2013. 362

3. Ibid, (Dewar, 2013, 362-364).

ABOUT THE AUTHOR

Michael W. Dewar, Sr. is a pastor, Bible teacher, and mentor in the spiritual life. He is also a Licensed Master Social Worker, and a specialist in resolution of conflicts, including church and family conflicts. He trains Agents of Peace-Managers of Conflict to launch peace ministries in local churches.

Reverend Dewar is the Founder and pastor of the New York Congregational Baptist Church ((NYCBC), and the author of several books, including a three-volume training course on *Church and Family Conflicts.*

He holds earned degrees from five institutions of higher learning, including the Master of Divinity from what is now Palmer Theological Seminary, Eastern University, the Master of Social Work from Wurzweiler School of Social Work, Yeshiva University, the LMSW from the State of New York, and a doctorate from Regent University, School of Divinity.

At the time of this publication, Reverend Dewar was pastoring in New York where he lives with his family.

RESURRECTION OF HUMANS

OTHER BOOKS BY THIS AUTHOR

Series: *"Related Events to the Second Coming of the Christ"*

Number of Books in Series:10. Add them to your reading list.

Volume 1   Volume 2

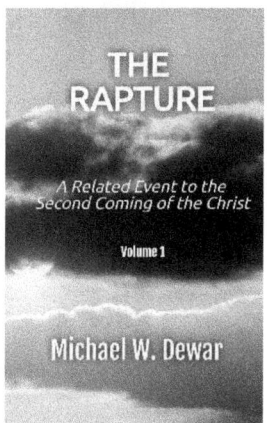

Volume 3

Volume 4

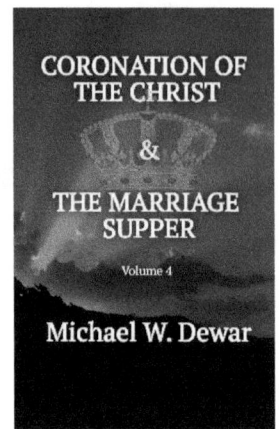

Volume 5

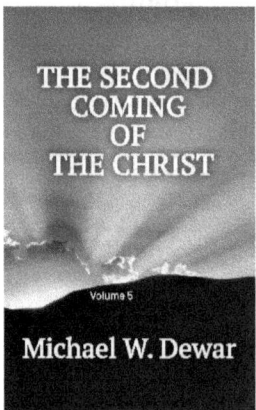

Volume 6

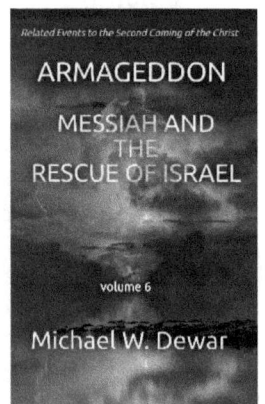

OTHER BOOKS BY THIS AUTHOR

Volume 7

Volume 8

Volume 9
The Final Judgment

Volume 10
The New World Order

These two are coming soon; the covers are temporary.

OTHER BOOKS BY THIS AUTHOR

BISCRA, a consumable not shown here, but designed to be used with the journal, may not be available. Check website: dpscleansing.com

How to Resolve Conflict by Establishing
A Peace Ministry in your Church

Textbook

Instructor's Manual   Students' Manual

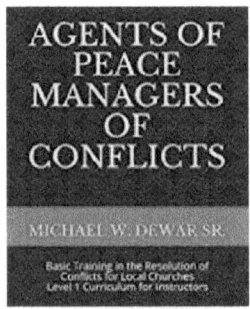   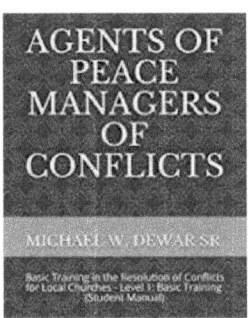

Training for agents of peace, managers of conflict.

OTHER BOOKS BY THIS AUTHOR

Is You Dwelling Place Spiritually Cleansed? Your Health and wellbeing may very well depend on this yearly Spiritual Exercise.

Learn How to Bless Your Home and Family

Free yourself from the curse and cursing.

OTHER BOOKS BY THIS AUTHOR

OTHER BOOKS BY THIS AUTHOR

BISCRA-40 is a consumable (may be unavailable)

OTHER BOOKS BY THIS AUTHOR

**Did You Know there will be a Believers Judgment?
It is a court appearance, learn how to prepare for it.**

**Did You Know Keep Record of Everybody?
Make Sure You are in the Right Book Up there.**

Second Edition

OTHER BOOKS BY THIS AUTHOR

First Edition

SIGNUP FOR NEWSLETTER

HERE OR AT:
THE DWELLING PLACE DPSCLEANSING.COM

Send Feedback to author at:

CS@DPSCLEANSING.COM

OTHER BOOKS BY THIS AUTHOR

RESURRECTION OF HUMANS

www.ingramcontent.com/pod-product-compliance
Lightning Source LLC
Chambersburg PA
CBHW071723040426
42446CB00011B/2189